YOUR KNOWLEDGE HAS VALUE

- We will publish your bachelor's and master's thesis, essays and papers

- Your own eBook and book - sold worldwide in all relevant shops

- Earn money with each sale

Upload your text at www.GRIN.com and publish for free

Bibliographic information published by the German National Library:

The German National Library lists this publication in the National Bibliography; detailed bibliographic data are available on the Internet at http://dnb.dnb.de .

Imprint:

Copyright © 2016 GRIN Verlag, Open Publishing GmbH
Print and binding: Books on Demand GmbH, Norderstedt Germany
ISBN: 9783668385931

This book at GRIN:

http://www.grin.com/en/e-book/351180/introduction-into-financial-accounting-according-to-ifrs

Mike G.

Introduction into Financial Accounting according to IFRS

GRIN Publishing

GRIN - Your knowledge has value

Financial Accounting

The following text was created as part of the university module "financial accounting according to IFRS standards". This work will introduce into the financial reporting procedure as well as into the legal framework and enable the reader to create (simple) financial statements by his/her own. Several examples and numerical figures support the understanding as well as visual displays. At the end a summary about the balance sheet adjustments as well as a kind of FAQ (as part of the exam preparation) is added. Be aware that the approaches are very similar to the German ones, but not always the same.

This work is made out of the notes from the lectures and supplemented by additional information and pictures out of the secondary literature "Financial Accounting – International financial reporting standards" published by Pearson and written by Walter T. Harrison Jr. and Charles T. Horngreen (**ISBN-13:** 978-0273777809). Additionally some information were visually displayed by self-made figures, diagrams and compilations. If an image is not marked differently, it's self-created.

Basics

- Accounting has a great problem, the incomparability of information.
  → Transformation of information is necessary.
- Accounting provides information by identifying, measuring, communicating, recording, classifying and summarizing of financial events and transactions.
- Many groups in and outside the company are interested in truth and transparent financial accounting.
  - **Company** itself for decision making, e.g., the use of scarce resources or prediction of opportunity costs.
    - **Employees** want to know the financial situation of the company, so they can calculate with retirement benefits, employment opportunities and so on.
  - **Suppliers** to evaluate the ability of the company to pay the supplied goods and interest in a long-term customer.
  - **State** for taxes and regulations.
  - **Public** for CSR, risk of pollution will lead to protest against this company.
  - **Consumers** have long term involvements (e.g. warranties) and need to know the continuance of the company.
  - **Shareholders** to evaluate the risk of giving money, determine whether to buy, hold or sell.
  - **Creditors** to evaluate the risk of lending money and height of interest rates.
    - As well as **information intermediaries** like rating agencies or financial analysts.
  - **Stakeholder** are interested in company, but not necessary hold shares.

- **Differences between financial and management accounting.**
  - **Financial accounting**: communication to the outside.
    - Following a general purpose, should give a generic overview, is highly regulated, once or twice a year, backward looking, providing information for buying, holding or selling shares.
  - **Management accounting**: for internal use only, decision making.

- Specific purpose, detailed information, not regulated, made for every single decision, forward looking.

- **Business Activities.**
  - **(1) Operating Activities.**
    - Daily processes (core values) for making money, depends what the company is.
    - Primary activities to provide the customers with goods and services to generate cash.
  - **(2) Investing Activities.**
    - Purchase and sell of all goods that produce other goods.
    - Buying something with the hope to receive more money back.
  - **(3) Financing Activities.**
    - Acquiring financial resources to engage in operating and investing activities.
    - Raising of capital or debt, e.g., trading at stock exchange markets.

- **Financial accounting statements.**
  - **(1) Statement of comprehensive income (I/S).**[1]
    - Comparison of company's revenue and expenses for a period.
    - Separated in two statements (Income Statement and Statement of other Com-prehensive Income) (Last one is not necessary for the exam).

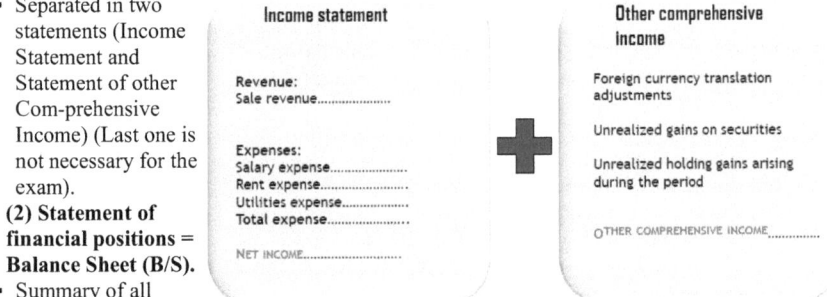

  - **(2) Statement of financial positions = Balance Sheet (B/S).**
    - Summary of all assets and source of capital, not for this period, contains information of all periods since the founding of the company.
    - Information for investors to see the development of an company as well as the debt ratio.
  - **(3) Statement of cash flow (CF).**
    - Providing all transactions of a company, which are related to real flow of cash.
    - Used to determine the cash on the bank account or the first position in the balance sheet.
    - Shows the liquidity of a company.
  - **(4) Statement of changes in Equity (ΔEq.).**
    - Reveals the changes in Equity and is used to check the calculated worth in the balance sheet.

- **Structure of a balance sheet.**[2]
  - Balance sheet is divided into two parts, use of funds on the left side, source of funds on the right.
  - **Assets = Liabilities + Equity.**
    - Sum of total assets has to be the same as sum of equity and liabilities.

---

1 picture taken from Financial Accounting by Walter T. Harrison Jr. and Charles T. Horngreen
2 picture taken from Financial Accounting by Walter T. Harrison Jr. and Charles T. Horngreen

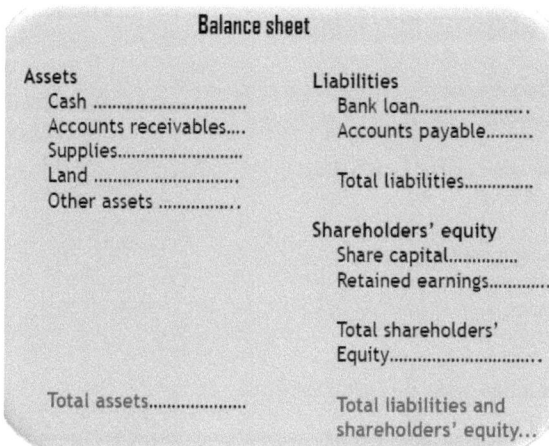

- **Components of retained earnings.**[3]
  - ○ Former value of retained earnings will be extended by the net income.
    - ▪ Net income is calculated in the statement of the comprehensive income.
    - ▪ Difference between revenues and expenses in one period.
  - ○ Sum of retained earnings and net income will be reduced by dividends to calculate the ending balance of retained earnings.

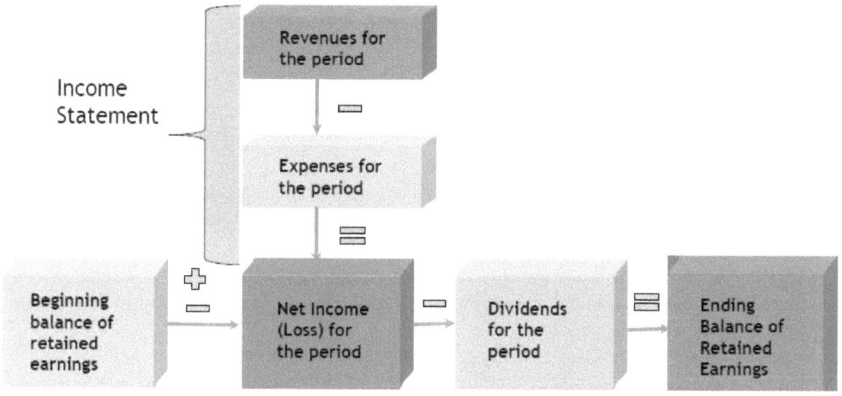

---

3   picture taken from Financial Accounting by Walter T. Harrison Jr. and Charles T. Horngreen

- **Structure of a cash flow statement.**[4]
  - **(I) Cash flow from operating activities.**
    - Net Income.
    - Adjustment to reconcile net income to net cash provided by operating activities (given in exam).
      => Net cash from operating activities.
  - **(II) Cash flow from investing activities.**
    - Acquisition of land.
    - Sale of land.
      => Net cash from investing activities.
  - **(III) Cash flow from financing activities.**
    - Issuance of shares.
    - Payment of dividends.
      => Net cash from financing activities.
  - **(IV) Total cash flow** is the sum of all three cash flows.

Cash flow statement

Cash flows from operating activities
Net income..7.300
Adj. ....(3.900)
Net cash from operating activities...3.400

Cash flows from investing activities
Acquisition of land.........................(40.000)
Sale of land 22.000
Net cash from investing activities (18.000)

Cash flows from financing activities
Issuance of share...............................50.000
Payment of dividends ....(2.100)
Net cash from financing activities... 47.900

Net increase in cash........................... 33.300
Cash balance, 31/12/2013 0
CASH BALANCE, 31/12/2014...............33.300

- **Statement of changes in equity.**[5]
  - Beginning Equity.
  - Issuance of share capital.
  - Net income.
  - Cash dividends.
    => Ending Equity.

Statement of changes in equity

BEGINNING EQUITY.................
Issuance of share capital
Net income...................
Cash dividends...............

ENDING EQUITY ....

- **Why the financial statement is made.**
  - Investors and Creditors need information whether to buy, sell, hold shares or lend money.
  - **Decision Usefulness**: Company has to reveal all information investors need for decision making.
  - Information have to represent the real situation of the company and have to be relevant.
    - Furthermore information has to be comparable, verifiable, understandable and accurate in time.
  - Fundamental qualities of the information are relevance and faithful representation.
    - **Relevance**: financial statement should reveal the actual value of the firm as well as a prognosis about the future value based on the goals and strategy.
    - **Faithful Representation**: financial statement should contain complete, neutral and error-free information.
  - **Scope of the f/s:** Should reveal as much information that a third party person is able to get a general overview about the company's financial situation.
  - **Goal of the f/s:** Permission of decision making for actual as well as potential investors.
  - **Fundamental Characteristics** of a f/s are Relevance and Reliability (Faithful Representation).
  - **Enhancing Characteristics** of f/s: Comparability, Verifiability, Timeliness, Understandability.

---

4 picture taken from Financial Accounting by Walter T. Harrison Jr. and Charles T. Horngreen
5 picture taken from Financial Accounting by Walter T. Harrison Jr. and Charles T. Horngreen

- **Relevance vs. Reliability.**
  - **Relevant information** contains every info may be having an influence on investors decision (degree of materiality); need to be revealed.
  - **Reliable information** contains (i) <u>every</u> information may be having an influence on investors behavior, (ii) won't give a party any unfair advantage, (iii) is free from error, (iv) reflect economic reality and (v) uses a certain degree of caution when predicting company's development.
  - Manager have to assess on reliability and relevance of any information, to avoid uncertainty and limit the power of managers three principles are set.
    - (I) Avoiding specific accounting treatment.
    - (II) Increasing disclosure (more information have to be revealed).
    - (III) Control mechanism (external auditors have to proof the financial reports).

- **Organizing a business.**
  - Three basic forms of companies.
  - **(1) Proprietorship**: One owner is personally liable.
  - **(2) Partnership**: Two or more partners, only general partners are liable.
  - **(3) Corporation**: Shareholders are owners and not personally liable.
  - → In the exam only the f/s from a corporation will be asked.

- **Transactions and Double-entry system.**
  - Transactions are changes within the company, e.g., the change of cash and bought assets.
  - Every transaction contains at least two information, necessary for the book-keeping.
  - → The first information is always (or should be) clear, the second have to be thought about.

- **What is a credit and a debit?**
  - Answer to question above depends on the side of the Balance Sheet.
  - A *debit* in <u>assets</u> mean an increase in worth, so a *credit* is an outflow of worth / a decrease.
  - A *debit* in <u>Liabilities</u> or <u>Equity</u> means a decrease of worth, because of repaying a loan or losing equity.
  - Example: Taking a bank loan increases the liabilities, so the "bank credit" is called credit.
    - Simultaneous the amount of cash on the asset-side increases, called a debit.
  - Important: Always think about the balance between sum of assets and sum of liabilities and equity; this sum must be kept even with the amount of credits and debits.
  - => Therefore: **If there is a credit, there need to be a debit with the same value.**

- **How to prepare a balance sheet starting with blank sheet of paper (Important Guideline).**
  - Companies will do a lot of transactions over the year, but every transaction is saved with date and sent to the accounting guys.
  - 1st **Step:** Making a journal out of the list with transactions.
  - 2nd **Step**: Turning the information from the journal into T-Accounts.
  - 3rd **Step**: Arrange the single T-Accounts into the ledger.
  - 4th **Step**: Turn information from ledger into a trial balance.
  - 5th **Step**: With the information of the trial balance you can start calculating the net income in the I/S
  - 6th **Step**: Closing the books for calculating retained earnings.
  - 7th **Step**: Calculating the total changes in Equity.
  - 8th **Step**: Start doing the Cash Flow Statement with all it's varies.
  - 9th **Step**: Finally, the B/S is ready to be made.

- **Step One: The journal.**
  - **Example**: Performing services on account leads to an *increase* in assets (account receivable), **debit** on asset's side.
    - Furthermore this will lead to a *increase* in retained earnings (service revenue → *increase* in net income → *increase* in retained earnings), so a **credit** on equity's side.

T1: Getting revenue on account for services.
first (obvious) information — accounts receivable
second (hidden) information — service revenue

Journal

Transacion number	Accounts & Explanation	Debit	Credit
T1	Acc. Rec.	●	
	Ser. Rev.		●

  - Analyze the given information and find out, what is the second (hidden) information and then decide what is a **debit** and what a **credit**.
    => Always begin with the debit account!
  - Normally the real capital volume is given (example above: Ser. Rev. in the height of $15k), so the capital will be inserted in the column **debit / credit**.
  - If it is directly asked in the exam, **only then** you have to write a short explanation under Ser. Rev. about the transaction ("revenue on account for services").
  - *Decreases* in capital aren't wrote in brackets or with minus, just put into the right field (**debit** or **credit**).

- **Step Two: The T-Accounts.**
  - Journal contains a huge amount of **debits** and **credits** for several accounts.
  - This step means sorting the **debits** or **credits** by their accounts.
  - **Example**: T2 and T5 both lead to an increase in cash (= **debit**), so they will be summarized in one T-Account.
    - **But**: T2 is connected to a sale of land, and T5 to issuance of shares; This information will be kept in two different T-Accounts, so for the transactions 2 and 5 we turned 4 information into three T-Accounts.
    - **Important**: Always begin with the debit side.
  - After filling the T-Accounts, notice the balance on the bottom.

Cash	
Debit	Credit
(T2) 15k	...
(T5) 7k	
...	

land		share capital issuance of shares	
Debit	Credit	Debit	Credit
...	(T2) 15k	...	(T5) 7k
	...		...

Cash	
Debit	Credit
(T2) 15k	
(T5) 7k	
Bal. 22k	

6

• Step Three: The Ledger.
- ○ In the ledger you sort the T-Accounts by their side of the B/S.
- ○ Don't forget to notice the Transaction number or date before the capital amount.
- ○ Order the companion accounts close to each other (salary payable close to salary payable; building close to building depreciation expenses, close to accumulated building depreciation).

Ledger

Assets   =   Liabilities   +   Shareholder's Equity

Cash

Debit	Credit
(T2) 15k	
(T5) 7k	
Bal. 22k	

land

Debit	Credit
	(T2) 15k
	Bal. 15k

share capital

Debit	Credit
	(T5) 7k
	Bal. 7k

• Step Four: The Trial Balance.
- ○ Now bring the single balances (not the T-Accounts anymore) into a nice order for the further steps.
- ○ The account title on the left will contain the balance in the right order (decreases in assets not negative, just in credit, as well as decreases in L&E).

Trial balance

Accounts title	Debit	Credit
Cash	22k	
Sales of land		5k
Share capital		7k

• Step Six: Closing the Books.[6]
- ○ Temporary accounts need to be "reset" for the next period.
- ○ Writing the same amount as the total ending balance on the other side (debit or credit) closes the book.
- ○ Because of doing this, you have to add the total ending balance of these accounts into the retained earnings account (on the "normal" side, expenses as debit, revenue as credit).

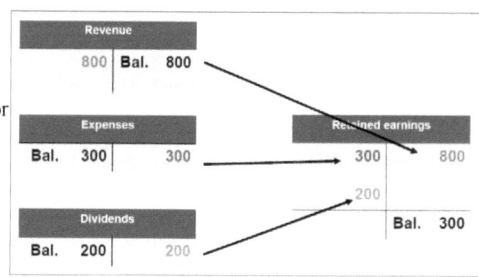

- ○ With this you can calculate the retained earnings.
  => Do not insert the new value of Retained Earnings in the trial balance! Use the old value.

• Distinction between accrual and cash-flow accounting.
- ○ Accrual accounting: When events occurring than the revenue will influence the net income.
- ○ Cash based accounting: Only when cash is moving, events will influence net income.
  => Accrual accounting is much better to measure the performance of companies.

• When a Revenue is Recognized.
- ○ Goods must change the owner; even if the goods are fully paid and left the seller, the goods only become property of the buyer if they arrive at his place.
  → Then the seller has realized a revenue.

---

6   picture taken from Financial Accounting by Walter T. Harrison Jr. and Charles T. Horngreen

- Only if the services are completely done the performer will realize revenue, even if the service was paid before performing.

- **The Matching Concept.**
- Every transaction will affect the balance sheet at least two times.
- Expenses or revenues influence the equity by changing retained earnings.

- **Adjustments.**
- Three kinds of adjustments need to be considered.
- **(1) Deferrals (Cash now, leisure later on).**
  - Company paid or received cash in advance and expect to get or do sth. in the future.
  - Bought supplies for cash now and later on the amount of supplies will decrease because of using them in the production process.
  - Getting cash for doing sth. will be accounted as unearned revenue, as the leisure is done, the amount of unearned revenue will decrease accordingly.
- **(2) Depreciation (Costs of PPE will be shared on PPE's lifetime).**
  - Common long-term deferral; PPE will lose value over the useful lifetime.
  - Machinery costs $ 10k and is expected to last 10 years until needing a new one.
  - Asset: Machinery has the value of $ 10k at the time of acquiring.
  - At the end of the year it lost $(\frac{total\ costs}{lifetime}) x \frac{months\ used}{12}$ in value.
  - At the end of next year it lost a constant yearly rate of value.
    => Supposed straight line depreciation!
- **(3) Accruals (Cash later, leisure now).**
  - Company bought or did something but the expense or revenue will come just later on.
  - Company bought some new land, but bill has to be paid in 2 weeks (account payable).
  - Company performed some service, but will receive cash in 2 weeks (account receivable).

- **Five categories of adjusting entries.**
- **(1) Prepaid expenses (deferral).**
  - Rent for the next three months is paid → cash is credited.
  - Next month the building was used → rent expense occurs and decrease prepaid rent's value.
  - **Special Case: Supplies.**
    - Acquiring supplies → cash decrease, supply increase.
    - Using supplies → increase supply expense, decrease supply.
- **(2) Depreciation of PPE (deferral).**[7]
  - Every PPE object has to be depreciated when the balance sheet is made.
    - Normally once a year, so there is an annual depreciation rate.
    - But in the year of acquisition the PPE object was only a few months in company, so the annually depreciation rate has to be reduced by monthly depreciation rate of "not-being-in-the-company"-time.
  - In the balance sheet depreciation will never reduce the value of assets directly.
    - Open two new accounts for those tasks.
    - **Depreciation expense** account contains the annual depreciation rate for this period.
    - **Accumulated depreciation** consists of the beginning depreciation balance and will be increased by the "this-year"-depreciation rate.

---

7   pictures taken from Financial Accounting by Walter T. Harrison Jr. and Charles T. Horngreen

Equipment			Accumulated depreciation - Equipment			Depreciation expense - Equipment		
Jun 3	24.000							
			Jun 30	400		Jun 30	400	
Bal.	24.000							
			Bal.	400		Bal.	400	

- In the balance sheet the value of one PPE object is given as well as the accumulated depreciation value and both will be totaled.
  - → It is important to show the initial value of the object as well as the sum of depreciation.

PP&E on Balance Sheet at June 30		
Equipment	€24.000	
Less: Accumulated depreciation	(400)	€23.600
Building	€50.000	
Less: Accumulated depreciation	(200)	€49.800
Carrying amount of PP&E		€73.400

- **(3) Unearned revenues (deferral).**
  - Getting cash before performing a service will create a liability named "unearned service revenue".
    - If the service is dividable and when a part of it is finished at the end of the accounting period, you have to adjust (in this case "reduce") the value of unearned service revenues by service revenue.
      - → It is not a pert of the income statement if its still a unearned service revenue.
- **(4) Accrued expenses (accrual).**
  - Company is preparing itself to face safe (not expected) expenses in the future.
  - Cash is not affected, but a salary expense will lead to a "salary payable" – liability.
- **(5) Accrued revenue (accrual).**
  - Performing a service but still don't get paid → account receivable.

- **Book Value vs. Market Value.**
  - **Market value** is the evaluated worth of an asset (or sth. else) determined by offer and demand.
  - **Book value** is the asset's cost and the accumulated depreciation (= **carrying amount**).

- **Depreciation, Amortization and Depletion – Triplets with the same meaning.**
  - Intangible Assets won't become depreciated, they will become amortized.
    - Software, Patents, Licenses etc.
    - Goodwill is the difference between the buying price for one company and the worth of it's net assets (assets – liabilities).
  - Natural Resources will become depleted.
    => Depletion and Amortization works in the same way depreciation works.

- **Assessing what is a PPE and what's it's value.**
  - PPE are fixed, long-lived and non-current assets, which are expected to be used more than one period → Costs of half-finished construction at the end of a period, Investment properties (real estate gaining rents) or Biological assets in agriculture.
    - Furthermore they were expected to generate future economic benefit and it's costs can be measured reliably.
  - Costs for purchasing and making ready are totaled and will be spread over the estimated lifetime.

◦ **Land as a PPE.**
- Freehold land is long-living, but won't decrease in value, so it won't be depreciated.
- Leasehold land has to be depreciated as normal, because the lifetime is finite.
- Costs of Land include purchase price, transaction costs (taxes, fees) and dismantling costs (demolishing an old building to build a new one, removing costs of rubbish).
- "Land Improvements" are a separate T-Account including costs to improve the land (fencing, security systems etc.).

- **Lump Sum Purchases.**
  ◦ Buying several assets for one lump sum (= combined, reduced) price.
  ◦ **Problem**: Assets has to be depreciated in different ways, e.g. the land and the building.
  ◦ **Relative-sales-value-method**: Searching for the market value of the single assets and calculate the relation between them.
  - With this relation, split the lump sum in that way and you received the costs for every single asset.

Bought land and building for a lump sum of 40.000 €		
	Relation	
Market value of building		Cost of building
- 30.000 €	60%	60 % of 40.000 = 24.000 €
Market value of land		Cost of land
- 20.000 €	40%	40% of 40.000 = 16.000 €

- **The Three Depreciation Methods.**
  ◦ **(1) Straight-line depreciation** – Used for assets that generate revenue annualy.
  - Depreciable costs are the purchasing / producing costs minus the estimated residual value ("Schrottwert").
  - Depreciable costs divided over the useful lifetime in years reveals the annual depreciation rate.
  - You need to estimate the useful lifetime as well as the residual value (given in the exam).
  -

Date	Depreciation rate	Depreciable amount	Depreciation expense	Accumulated Depreciation	Asset Carrying Amount
01.01.16					35000
31.12.16	0,33	30000	10000	10000	25000
31.12.17	0,33	30000	10000	20000	15000
31.12.18	0,33	30000	10000	30000	5000

  ◦ **(2) Units-of-production depreciation** – Used for assets that wear out because of usage.
  - Depreciable cost divided over useful lifetime In units leads to the depreciation rate per unit.
  - Depreciation rate per unit is multiplied with the activity for every period.
  - You need to estimate the useful lifetime as well as the number of units (given in the exam).

Date	Depreciation rate per unit	Number of units	Depreciation expense	Accumulated Depreciation	Asset Carrying Amount
01.01.16					25000
31.12.16	0,4	15000	6000	6000	
31.12.17	0,4	5000	2000	8000	
31.12.18	0,4	35000	14000	22000	3000

- ◦ **(3) Double-declining-balance depreciation** – Used for assets losing more value in the first years.
  - ▪ DDB rate is the costs (within the residual value) divided through the years of useful lifetime and subsequently multiplied with 2.
  - ▪ DDB rate will be multiplied with the book value first and than with the carrying amount.
  - ▪ You need to estimate the residual value as well as the useful lifetime (given in the exam).
  - ▪ The last depreciation rate is a "plug", will depreciate as much as needed to reach the residual value at the end of lifetime.
  - ▪ If the carrying amount is fallen below the estimated residual value before the last year, this year's depreciation rate will become the "plug" and in the other years won't be depreciated.
  - ▪

Date	DDB rate	Asset Carrying Amount	Depreciation expense	Accumulated Depreciation	Asset Carrying Amount
01.01.16					25000
31.12.16	0,4	25000	10000	10000	15000
31.12.17	0,4	15000	6000	16000	9000
31.12.18		9000	3000	19000	6000

- • **When to capitalize or to expense.**
  - ◦ A **expense** occurs normally from the day-to-day servicing.
    - ▪ A car repair or maintenance is normal for a car, so this is a expense.
  - ◦ A **carrying amount** occurs if special investments in PPE are done.
    - ▪ Regularly occurring costs that are necessary to improve / keep the worth of an asset like a new part of the engine for an airplane can be capitalized too.
  - ◦ **Expenses** will reduce the net income directly, **carrying accounts** will affect the net income not so bad, but long-term.
    => Capital expenditures increasing the asset's capacity pr extend it's useful lifetime will be added to the asset's account.

- **Changes in estimates.**
  - If an asset is estimated to life 5 years long, the depreciation rate will be 5.000 €.
  - After 2 years this estimate turns out to be wrong, the asset is able to life 6 years.
  - Do not touch the previous depreciation rates or accumulated depreciation!
  - After recognizing this mistake, use the carrying amount to calculate a new rate of depreciation for the following years.
  -

30.000 / 5 years = annual depreciation rate of 6.000 €
18.000 / 4 years = annual depreciation rate of 4.500 €

Date	Depreciation rate	Depreciation amount	Depreciation expense	Accumulated Depreciation	Asset Carring Amount
01.01.16					30000
31.12.16	0,2	30000	6000	6000	24000
31.12.17	0,2	30000	6000	12000	18000
31.12.18	0,2	18000	4500	16500	13500
31.12.19	0,2	18000	4500	21000	9000
31.12.20	0,2	18000	4500	25500	4500
31.12.21	0,2	18000	4500	30000	0

- **Subsequent Measurements of PPE.**
  - Two methods are allowed and you are allowed to switch them.
  - **(1) Cost Method.**
    - The initial costs of PPE determined the beginning book value of the asset reduced by depreciation and impairment.
    - Book value has to be lower than or equal to recoverable value (if you sell it or use it to the end).
  - **(2) Revaluation Method.**
    - Value of assets is determined by fair value (market price / value).
      - Depreciation and impairment also decline the asset's value.
  - Switch from common cost method to revaluation method if fair value is higher to receive a greater balance sum.
  - Condition to switch: You have to be able to safely measure the fair value.
  - Guideline in the Ledger for switching to revaluation method.
    - Asset carrying amount is 100 at the end of year 2, fair value 120.
    - The difference is a revaluation adjustment handled as an expense, but not relevant in the normal Income Statement.

PPE was bought 2 years ago for 150, estimated to life 6 years long.
Now fair value is 120   Revaluation

PPE		Acc Dep		Adjustment
150	30	50	50	20

  - When changing the method, the depreciation will began again, so the initial worth of the PPE has to be like the fair value is (decrease of assets value).
    - In addition to this the progress of depreciation has to be "reset" by debiting the accumulated depreciation.

- **The Impairment Test.**
  - ◦ Have to be done at least each year, you can either pass it or fail it.
  - ◦ Check whether book value is higher (failed!) or lower the recoverable amount.
  - ◦ **Guideline.**
    - ▪ (1) Compare the two possible recoverable amounts (calculation scroll down).
    - ▪ (2) Compare the higher one (value in use vs. fair value less costs to sell) with the book value (carrying amount).
    - ▪ (3) If the book value is higher (and the test fails), you have to compute an impairment loss like a depreciation expense (difference between book value and recoverable value).

- **How to determine fair value less costs to sell.**
  - ◦ Fair value is given in the exam.
  - ◦ Fair value is the price of the asset in a binding sale agreement.
    - ▪ If there is no sale agreement, you have to look at the market, either the current bid price or the price of the most recent transaction.
    - • In any other case the fair value based on the best information available, comparing with similar assets within the same industry.

- **How to determine the value in use / present value.**
  - ◦ Not given in the exam, we have to calculate it out of the following data.
    - ▪ (1) Estimated future cash flows.
    - ▪ (2) Estimated future selling price.
    - ▪ (3) Number of periods.
    - ▪ (4) Discount rate (interest rate for the time value of money).
  - ◦ $Calculation: PV = P*[\dfrac{1-(1+r)^{-n}}{r}] + SP*(1+r)^{-n}$

with
PV = Present Value
P = Cash Flow
r = Interest Rate
n = Periods
SP = Selling Price

- **Gains and losses on sale of PPE.**[8]
  - ◦ Impairment losses will be handled as expenses in the I/S.
  - ◦ Selling such assets instead of computing a impairment loss will receive a gain / loss which were also handled as expenses in the I/S.

Sep 30	Cash	7,300	
	Accumulated Depreciation	3,750	
	Equipment		10,000
	Gain on sale of PPE		1,050
	To sell equipment		

  - ◦ Revaluation adjustments are reported as gains in other comprehensive income, not in the I/S.
    - • Accounting principle told to be cautions when evaluating the worth of assets.
    - • Better a lower value, than a higher one.
    - • If assets were sold, the value was clear → I/S
    - • If assets were expected to gain more money → not into the I/S because its just an expectation.

---

8   picture taken from Financial Accounting by Walter T. Harrison Jr. and Charles T. Horngreen

- **What are intangible assets?**
  - Four characteristics of intangible assets.
    - **(1) Identifiable**: It has to be separable from the entity and could be sold.
    - **(2) Non-monetary**: No right to receive an amount of currency (future, e.g.).
    - **(3) Asset**: Future economic benefit is expected.
    - **(4) Without physical substance.**
  - They will be recorded at its acquisition costs.
  - Intangible assets can also be valued under cost or revaluation method, but only if the fair value can be measured reliably.
  - Intangible assets with an infinite live can't be amortized, but has to do annually impairment tests (e.g. goodwill).
  - Finite ones will be amortized and have to do impairment tests, too.
    - **Amortization**: straight line depreciation without residual value.

- **When to capitalize or expense intangible assets?**
  - **Four recognition criteria.**
    - (1) Identifiability.
    - (2) Control of the resource.
    - (3) Probability of future economic benefits.
    - (4) Reliable measurement of cost.
      => Only if all of the four criteria are fulfilled, the costs of intangible assets can be capitalized.
  - **Research phase**: A company can't prove whether an initial project will generate a probable future economic benefit.
  - **Development phase**: Advanced step in developing an intangible asset, company can prove that this will generate probable future economic benefits.
    => If research and development activities can't be separated clearly, than capitalization is not allowed.
  - If purchasing an intangible asset, than it can be capitalized.
  - **Internally generated intangible assets.**
    - Brands, customer lists or sth. like this can't be distinguished from the costs of developing the business as a whole → Research costs are always an expense.
    - Six criteria of when to capitalize development costs of internally generated intangible assets.
      - (1) Technical feasibility.
      - (2) Intention to complete the intangible asset.
      - (3) Ability to use or sell the intangible.
      - (4) Proof of how the intangible asset will generate probable future economic benefit.
      - (5) Availability of adequate resources (technical, financial) to complete the development.
      - (6) Ability to measure reliable the expenditures for the development of the intangible assets.
      => If all those six criteria are fulfilled, the development costs can be capitalized.

- **Goodwill.**[9]
  - Company B purchases Company A for 10 million.

Assets at fair value	€9,000,000
Goodwill	**3,000,000**
Liabilities	2,000,000
Cash	10,000,000

    - Company A owns assets with book value of 15, fair value 9; liabilities in the height of 5, fair value 2.
    - Goodwill is the difference of purchasing price and net assets (fair value of assets minus fair value of liabilities).
      → Goodwill contains 3 million, won't be amortized, but has to do impairment tests.

---

9   picture taken from Financial Accounting by Walter T. Harrison Jr. and Charles T. Horngreen

14

- Only goodwill from purchasing companies is allowed to be recorded, not internally generated goodwill, because it can't be measured reliably.
- Bargain purchase is a "negative goodwill" and goes into the Income Statement.
- **Goodwill is an asset in the balance sheet.**

- **Inventory.**[10]
  - Goods ready to be sold, but isn't yet.
  - If goods were sold, the revenue goes into the income statement as well as the costs of those goods sold.
  -

Journal			
Date	Accounts and explanation	Debit	Credit
	Inventory	560,000	
	Accounts payable		560,000
	Purchased inventory on account		
	Cost of goods sold	540,000	
	Inventory		540,000
	Recorded cost of goods sold		

Only the costs of the sold goods will be inserted in the income statement, not the costs of produced and stored ones.

Inventory

€100,000	540,000
560,000	
120,000	

Cost of Goods Sold

€540,000

10 pictures taken from Financial Accounting by Walter T. Harrison Jr. and Charles T. Horngreen

- **Inventory Costs.**
  - **(1) Value of Inventory.**[11]
    - Value of inventory is determined by purchase price, taxes, import duties and every cost needed to prepare the good to be sold.

Inventory	1,000	
Accounts payable		1,000
Purchase of inventory on 2/10, n/30 terms		

    - Other costs like advertising and sales commission are selling expenses.

Accounts payable	1,000	
Cash		980
Inventory		20
Payment of inventory on 2/10 settlement discount		

    - Trade discounts, rebates and anything similar must be deducted from the inventory value.
  - **(2) Purchase Returns.**
    - If the good is damaged and you want to hand it back to the supplier, than the former inventory increase will be decreased and the cash is increased by the money getting back from the supplier (not the same like the paid amount (taxes, import duties)).
      → Giving goods back and get (a part of the) cash back.
  - **(3) Purchase Allowance.**
    - Good is damaged, but buyer doesn't want to hand goods back; instead he/she wants to get some money back (an allowance).
    - Decrease in inventory's value, increase in cash.

- **Inventory Methods.**[12]
  - If buying the same goods several times in one period for different prices and only sold some of them, how much is the rest's value?
  - **(1) FIFO: First In – First Out.**
    - The first sold good is the first one bought; if four goods stored and three were sold, the last one purchased will remain in the storage.

  purchase order

  | 1 | 2 | 3 | 4 |

  3 ones were sold

  | 1 | 2 | 3 | CoGS |
  | 4 | | | Inventory |

  - **(2) LIFO: Last In – First Out.**
    - The first good purchased will be sold last, so in the example above good 1 will remain in the inventory and goods 4, 3 and 2 were sold.
  - **(3) Average Costs.**
    - Costs of all available units (inventory + purchases) over number of all available units reveals the average costs for every unit.
    - Similar to this the CoGS are the number of goods sold multiplied with the average costs.
    - The ending inventory is valued with number of units on hand multiplied with average costs.

---

11 picture taken from Financial Accounting by Walter T. Harrison Jr. and Charles T. Horngreen
12 pictures taken from Financial Accounting by Walter T. Harrison Jr. and Charles T. Horngreen

Increasing inventory prices			Decreasing inventory prices		
	Cost of goods sold	Ending inventory		Cost of goods sold	Ending inventory
FIFO	Lowest because based on older costs, which are less expensive	Highest because based on more recent and expensive costs	FIFO	Highest because based on older costs, which are more expensive	Lowest because based on more recent, less expensive costs
LIFO	Highest because based on more recent costs, which are more expensive	Lowest because based on older costs, which are less expensive	LIFO	Lowest because based on more recent costs which are less expensive	Highest because based on older, more expensive costs

○ **Why LIFO is not allowed under IFRS?**
- Conceptual framework from IFRS-Principles favors FIFO.
- No reliable representation of the company's actual inventory flows.
  → Lack of representation faithfulness.
- No good idea, not logical / rational / real.

• **Principles related to Inventories.**
  ○ **(1) Comparability Principle.**
  - You should use the same inventory method to enable investors comparing the inventory.
  - Method can be changed, than you have to disclosure the effect on net income related to changing the method.
    => You can change the method, but the old one has to be done anyway.
  ○ **Net Realizable Value.**
  - Impairment test for inventory, important for example if inventory is damaged.
  - Write down inventory value if estimated selling price is under the book value.
    • "Write down" is no extra journal entry, its just handled as a CoGS.

Cost of goods sold	600	
Inventory		600
Wrote inventory down to realizable amount		

- **Doubtful receivables.**
  - If you expect that accounts receivable won't be paid back in full amount or if its impossible for the debtor to pay it back because he/she is bankrupt, you have to decrease accounts receivable.
  - **(1) Allowance Method** – expectation.
    - Given probability of bankruptcy and credit accounts receivable.
      - A new t-account will be opened, the allowance for uncollectible receivable, which is related to an expense in the income statement.
    - Entry in the balance sheet will look like this.

Accounts receivable	10.000	
Less: Allowance for uncollectible receivables	.(900)	
Accounts receivables, net		9.100

- How to get the percentage for calculating the allowance.
  - In the exam percentages were given, first of all we have to credit an allowance if an account receivable is debited.
  - If the account receivable lasts longer than the accounting period, than you have to look how long the account receivable is outstanding and with the given percentage you have to calculate the ending balance.
    → Ending Balance minus existing allowance = another increase in allowance.
    => Make the accounts balance.

Accounts receivable			Allowance for doubtful receivables	Doubtful receivable expense		Service revenue	
10.000			100	100			10.000
			1.900	1.900			
			Bal. 2.000	Bal. 2.000			

  - If the account receivable occurs, than you have to credit an allowance of 1%.
  - If the account receivable still exists at the end of the financial period, than the ending balance has to fit with the percentage of allowance.
    → 20% of 10k is 2k, so crediting 1.9k more to get an ending balance of 2k.
  - If some amount of the account receivable was paid during the year, the allowance starts from 0 again, will be "reset".
    - If the debtor is gone bankrupt, you have to write off the remaining account receivable.

Accounts receivable		Allowance for doubtful receivables	
10000	900	900	2000
Bal 9.100			Bal. 1.100

→ Only the allowance is an expense, the write off don't!

18

- What if debtor will become able to pay the account receivable again
- **Method one**: Reverse the write-off.

Accounts receivable		Allowance for doubtful receivables	
10000	900	900	2000
900			900
Bal. 10.000			Bal. 2.00

- **Method two**: Debit cash, credit uncollectible expense.

Cash		Doubtful receivable expense	
900			900

- ○ **(2) Direct write-off method** – bankrupt has happened.
  - Wait until the accounts receivable really can't be paid and than write-off.

2011			
.Jan 31	Uncollectible-Account expense	12	
	Account receivable - Brown		9
	Account receivable - Fiesta		3
Wrote off bad debts by direct write off-method			

- Direct write-off method is not allowed under IFRS.
  - Its against the principle of cautioness, you must show investors what you expect to enable a new decision making process.

General Questions about the IFRS

1) What is the Conceptual Framework?
The conceptual framework is a guideline for Accountants to see which information the financial statements have to reveal and which can be left out. It is built up like the following:
Decision Usefulness is the major principle, the fundamental qualities are the relevance and reliability and finally the enhancing qualities were comparability, timeliness, verifiability and understandability

2) When did IFRS become mandatory in European countries?
1. January 2005

3) What are the scope and objective of IAS 1?
Revealing all information related to the financial situation of the own company to enable (potential) investors and stakeholders to get a general overview of the company's situation and make the best decisions possible

4) What are the fundamental and enhancing qualities of financial statements?
Fundamental qualities are relevance (what to reveal) and reliability (faithful representation of the company's financial situation).

5) How can managerial discretion be contained in the trade-off between relevance and reliability?
The IFRS increased disclosure, restricted special accounting treatments and introduced control

mechanisms (like external accountants examining the financial statements) to prevent fraud by managers.

6) According to which principle is revenue recognized?
According to IAS 18 the revenue is only allowed to be recognized if the service is performed completely or the purchased goods were delivered and accepted by the buyer (not just delivered). In all other cases either an unearned service revenue / unearned sales revenue is computed or nothing if no money is received yet.

7) List some of the items that appear under "other comprehensive income".
- Revaluation adjustment
- Gains/losses from foreign currencies

8) What is the content of an audit report?
Prove of the information in the financial statement were true, questionable or intentionally wrong

9) What is the definition of current asset?
Will leave the company in less than one accounting period.

Summary Adjustments

- (1) Impairment Test.
- (2) Net Realizable Value.
- (3) Revaluation Adjustments.
- (4) Depreciation // Amortization // Disposal.
- (5) Changes in Estimates.
- (6) Goodwill.
- (7) Recording Inventory.
- (8) Deferrals.
- (9) Accruals.
- (10) Doubtful receivables.

- **Impairment Test.**
  - Have to be done at least each year, you can either pass it or fail it.
  - Check whether book value is higher (failed!) or lower the recoverable amount.
  - **Guideline.**
    - (1) Compare the two possible recoverable amounts (fair value or present value).
    - (2) Compare the higher one (value in use vs. fair value less costs to sell) with the book value (carrying amount).
    - (3) If the book value is higher (and the test fails), you have to compute an impairment loss like a depreciation expense (difference between book value and recoverable value).
  - **Journal Entry – example.**

Impairment loss	2.040	
Accumulated impairment losses		2.040

- **Balance Sheet – example.**

Machinery	10000	
LESS: Accumulated depreciation	.(5000)	
LESS: Accumulated impairment loss	.(2040)	
Assets Carrying Amount		2.960

- **Net Realizable Value.**
  - Impairment test for inventory, important for example if inventory is damaged.
  - "Write down" inventory if book value is higher than the expected selling price is no extra journal entry, its just handled as a CoGS.
    - **Journal Entry – example.**

Cost of good sold	600	
Inventory		600
Revaluation of Inventory (2.000 – 600)		

  - **Balance Sheet – example.**

Inventory	1.400

- **Revaluation Adjustment.**
  - Is the market price (much) higher than the book value, you can decide to adjust the book value to the fair value.
  - Condition to switch: You have to be able to safely measure the fair value.
  - Revaluation Adjustment is not included in the Income Statement.
  - Accumulated depreciation will be "reset", Adjustment has to be revealed in the annex.
  - **Journal Entry – example.**

Accumulated depreciation	50	
Revaluation Adjustment		20
PP&E		30
Revalued PPE from book value 100 (150 – 50) to 120		

  - **Balance Sheet – example.**

PP&E	120
Retained Earnings	20

- **Depreciation // Amortization // Disposal.**
  - Spread the costs of purchase over the useful lifetime.
  - **(a) Straight-line depreciation.**
    - Calculate the inverse of the useful lifetime to get the depreciation rate.
    - Depreciation will be the same all over the time and reduce the assets carrying amount.
    - Attention: The depreciable amount is the historical cost minus residual value.
  - **(b) Units-of-production depreciation.**
    - Depreciation rate per unit has to be calculated by dividing the net asset carrying amount by the amount of useful units.
    - Depreciation rate will be multiplied by annual "used" units.
  - **(c) Double-declining-balance depreciation.**

- DDB rate will be the double one form straight line.
- DDB rate will be multiplied with annual assets carrying amount.
- Depreciation rate will be inserted in the Income Statement.
- **Journal Entry – example.**

Depreciation expense PP&E	1.000	
Accumulated depreciation PP&E		1.000
Annual depreciation rate for PP&E		

- **Balance Sheet – example.**

PP&E	10.000	
LESS: Accumulated depreciation	.(1.000)	
Asset carrying amount		9.000

- **Changes in Estimates.**
- If the useful lifetime of one PP&E is estimated for 10 years and after 5 years it is clear, that the PP&E will only last 2 years longer.
- Do not touch the accumulated depreciation account, just do another, new depreciation schedule and add the new depreciation costs to the old accumulated depreciation account.
- Only thing that changes is the annual depreciation expense, journalized in the same way as normal depreciation.

- **Goodwill.**
- If one company acquires another one, than you have to calculate the goodwill.
  - Goodwill = purchasing price – net assets (fair value of assets – fair value of liabilities).
  - Shareholder's equity is neglected in the exam (too complicated).
- If the goodwill is an bargain purchase, than you have to credit it, no longer an asset, just a gain, inserted into the Income Statement.
- **Journal Entry – example.**

Assets fair value	9m	
Goodwill	3m	
Liabilities		2m
Cash		10m
Purchasing company A for 10 million		

Assets fair value	9m	
Gain on bargain purchase		2m
Liabilities		2m
Cash		5m
Purchasing company A for 5 million		

○ **Balance Sheet – example.**

Goodwill	3m
Assets	Beginning balance + 9m
Liabilities	Beginning balance + 2m

○ Goodwill is an intangible asset and has to do impairments tests annually.
○ Fair value is given in the exam, can't be measured now.
○ **Journal Entry – example.**

Impairment loss on goodwill	2m	
Goodwill		2m
Goodwill is adjusted from 3m to 1m		

○ **Balance Sheet – example.**

Goodwill	3m	
LESS: Accumulated impairment losses	(2m)	
Asset carrying amount		1m

• **Recording Inventory.**
○ (a) Recording CoGS.
▪ If you produce your own inventory, than the CoGS have to be reduced only when the inventory is sold.
▪ If you purchase inventory, the CoGS have to be reduced immediately.
○ **Journal Entry – example.**

Inventory	560	
Cash		560
Purchased inventory in cash		
Cost of good sold	540	
Inventory		540
Recorded cost of good sold		

• CoGS is inserted into the Income Statement.
○ CoGS also concludes costs to make the inventory sellable (packaging etc.) or to receive the goods (import duties, taxes).
• CoGS were determined with FIFO or the Average cost method.

- Purchase settlements (reduced prices) will adjust the Inventory value.
  - **Journal Entry – example.**

Inventory	1000	
Accounts payable		1000
Purchased inventory on account payable		
Accounts payable	1000	
Cash		980
Inventory		20
Paid for inventory, received a 2% settlement discount		

  - **Balance Sheet – example.**

Inventory	980

- **Deferrals.**
  - Getting the cash now before doing or selling something.
  - Credit unearned service revenue and debit it if service is performed (even partly).
  - **Journal Entry – example.**

Cash	50	
Unearned Service Revenue		50
Received 50 in cash in advance		
Unearned Service Revenue	20	
Service Revenue		20
Performed 40% of the commissioned task		

  - Other important things were the prepaid expenses (specially for lease).
  - You have to specify this expense e.g. rent expense, leasing expense etc.
  - If the reason for those expenses occurs (even partly) you have to credit the prepaid expense and debit the related expense.

  - **Journal Entry – example.**

Prepaid Expense	50	
Cash		50
Paid cash in advance		
Expense	25	
Prepaid Expense		25
Half of the expense became due		

  - **Balance Sheet – example.**

Unearned service revenue (Liability)	20
Prepaid expense (Asset)	25

24

- **Accruals.**
  - Performing a service or selling a good, but receive cash later.
  - Important things were accrued expenses and accrued revenues.
  - Related t-accounts were accounts payable and accounts receivable because you have to reveal all definite events leading to cash decreases or increases.
    → If you have to pay monthly salary only a few weeks after you have to do the Balance Sheet, than you have to notice a salary payable because this expense will surely happen.
  - **Journal Entry – example.**

Salary expense	900	
Salary payable		900
Facing a salary payment in the near future		
Salary payable	900	
Cash		900
Expense occured and was paid in cash		

  - **Journal Entry – example.**

Account receivable	200	
Service revenue		200
Performed service on account		
Cash	50	
Account receivable		50
Customer paid 25%		

  - **Balance Sheet – example (if not paid yet).**

Account payable (Liability)	900
Account receivable (Asset)	200

- **(10) Doubtful Receivables.**
  - You can't expect every account receivable to be paid.
  - Some customers can not pay their debts, so a percentage "reduction" will be done, to show investors about the risks.
  - Allowance is related to a doubtful expense, decreasing the net income.
    → Expect insolvency from creditors.
  - Only if creditors gone bankrupt, than the accounts receivable will be write-off.
  - **Journal Entry – example.**

Account receivable	100	
Service Revenue		100
Performing revenue on account		
Doubtful receivable expense	1	
Allowance for doubtful receivables		1
Calculating the risk of not getting paid		

- **Journal Entry – example.**

Allowance for doubtful receivables	10	
Account receivable		10
Creditor isn't able to pay his bills anymore		
Doubtful receivable expense	9,9	
Allowance for doubtful receivables		9,9
"Refilled" the allowance account		

- Increase for 9,9, because the ending balance has to be 1% of the remaining accounts receivable
  → Decreased from 100 to 90, so 0,9 is the ending balance.

- **Balance Sheet – example.**

Accounts receivable	90	
LESS: Allowance for doubtful receivables	0,9	
Accounts receivable, net		89,1